NATIVE AMERICAN LANGUAGES

Bethanne Kelly Patrick

MASON CREST
PHILADELPHIA

NATIVE AMERICAN LIFE

NATIVE AMERICAN LANGUAGES

Bethanne Kelly Patrick

SENIOR CONSULTING EDITOR DR. TROY JOHNSON
PROFESSOR OF HISTORY AND AMERICAN INDIAN STUDIES
CALIFORNIA STATE UNIVERSITY

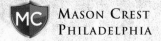

MASON CREST
PHILADELPHIA

Mason Crest
450 Parkway Drive, Suite D
Broomall, PA 19008
www.masoncrest.com

Printed and bound in the United States of America.

CPSIA Compliance Information: Batch #NAR2013. For further information, contact Mason Crest at 1-866-MCP-Book

First printing
1 3 5 7 9 8 6 4 2

Library of Congress Cataloging-in-Publication Data

Patrick, Bethanne Kelly.
Native American languages / Bethanne Kelly Patrick.
     pages cm. — (Native American life)
Includes bibliographical references and index.
ISBN 978-1-4222-2972-9 (hc)
ISBN 978-1-4222-8859-7 (ebook)
1. Indians of North America—Languages—Juvenile literature.
I. Title.
PM206.P37 2013
497—dc23
                                        2013007467

Native American Life series ISBN: 978-1-4222-2963-7

Frontispiece: Native American horsemen send a smoke signal from a rocky outcrop by waving a bundle of smoldering twigs in the air. Many tribes had distinct and creative ways of communicating.

TABLE OF CONTENTS

INTRODUCTION

For hundreds of years the dominant image of the Native American has been that of a stoic warrior, often wearing a full-length eagle feather headdress, riding a horse in pursuit of the buffalo, or perhaps surrounding some unfortunate wagon train filled with innocent west-bound American settlers. Unfortunately there has been little written or made available to the general public to dispel this erroneous generalization. This misrepresentation has resulted in an image of native people that has been translated into books, movies, and television programs that have done little to look deeply into the native worldview, cosmology, and daily life. Not until the 1990 movie *Dances with Wolves* were native people portrayed as having a human persona. For the first time, native people could express humor, sorrow, love, hate, peace, and warfare. For the first time native people could express themselves in words other than "ugh" or "Yes, Kemo Sabe." This series has been written to provide a more accurate and encompassing journey into the world of the Native Americans.

When studying the native world of the Americas, it is extremely important to understand that there are few "universals" that apply across tribal boundaries. With over 500 nations and 300 language groups the worlds of the Native Americans were diverse. The traditions of one group may or may not have been shared by neighboring groups. Sports, games, dance, subsistence patterns, clothing, and religion differed—greatly in some instances. And although nearly all native groups observed festivals and ceremonies necessary to insure the renewal of their worlds, these too varied greatly.

Of equal importance to the breaking down of old myopic and stereotypic images is that the authors in this series credit Native

Americans with a sense of agency. Contrary to the views held by the Europeans who came to North and South America and established the United States, Canada, Mexico, and other nations, some Native American tribes had sophisticated political and governing structures— that of the member nations of the Iroquois League, for example. Europeans at first denied that native people had religions but rather "worshiped the devil," and demanded that Native Americans abandon their religions for the Christian worldview. The readers of this series will learn that native people had well-established religions, led by both men and women, long before the European invasion began in the 16th and 17th centuries.

Gender roles also come under scrutiny in this series. European settlers in the northeastern area of the present-day United States found it appalling that native women were "treated as drudges" and forced to do the men's work in the agricultural fields. They failed to understand, as the reader will see, that among this group the women owned the fields and scheduled the harvests. Europeans also failed to understand that Iroquois men were diplomats and controlled over one million square miles of fur-trapping area. While Iroquois men sat at the governing council, Iroquois clan matrons caucused with tribal members and told the men how to vote.

These are small examples of the material contained in this important series. The reader is encouraged to use the extended bibliographies provided with each book to expand his or her area of specific interest.

Dr. Troy Johnson
Professor of History and American Indian Studies
California State University

1 Chief Seattle and the Lushootseed Language

The six-year-old boy hid in the reeds near his home camp to watch the unknown vessel approach. The year was 1792, and the place was an island harbor in the Puget Sound. The boy was a member of the Suquamish tribe of the Salish Indian people, named Sealth (pronounced SEE-elth). Sealth's father, Schweabe, was the *tyœ*, or chief, of the Suquamish tribe, who lived on what is now Bainbridge Island.

Sealth lived in a world that had not seen outsiders for decades, if ever. The Salish Indians occupied area in the Pacific Northwest that is among the most fertile and temperate of the continent. Heavily wooded lands and rainy weather meant that the Salish people could hunt game, such as deer and bear, fish for plentiful salmon, and harvest the many fruits that flourish in the region.

A statue of Chief Seattle stands near the Seattle Center in Washington State. Chief Seattle was the leader of the Suquamish people at the time Europeans began to colonize the Northwest coast.

Sealth's mother, Politza, was the daughter of a Duwamish chieftain. However, children lived with their father's people, which is why Sealth lived on Suquamish lands.

While Sealth's tribe lived in huts that looked poor and inadequate to European explorers, the tribe had enough for its needs.

The unknown vessel approaching a harbor at Bainbridge Island was the H.M.S. *Discovery*, commanded by Captain George Vancouver. Vancouver, whose name would one day be given to one of Canada's largest cities, set anchor within view of Sealth, whose name would later be given to an important U.S. city.

The sight of an 18th-century English sailing ship must have been mind-boggling to a boy who lived in a bark-and-branch hut. Sealth would have seen the huge construction of wood, metal, and cloth and wondered where it had come from. He would have watched men with pale skin and complicated clothing unload guns and other supplies from the vessel's sides. He would have heard shouts in a strange language, made even stranger because everyone in his world would have spoken the Salish dialect Lushootseed.

Historians don't know much about Sealth's thoughts on his sighting of Vancouver's ship and its contents, both human and material. The little they do know comes from late-19th-century recollections of Suquamish tribal elders. Later in his life, Sealth spoke often and with pleasure about seeing the *Discovery*.

However little we know of what Sealth saw and thought, the

Curious natives paddle out to witness the evacuation of the H.M.S. *Discovery* in Queen Charlotte's Sound. The ship became caught on rocks near the coast of British Columbia, and the captain, George Vancouver, was forced to abandon the ship.

NATIVE AMERICAN LIFE

encounter itself is a powerful example of "first contact." First contact means an initial encounter between two cultures. Often, one culture or civilization will be considerably more sophisticated than the other in terms of what it knows of the rest of the world. This was the case when Sealth saw Vancouver's ship: the Europeans had done a great

An island and a settlement in British Columbia were named after George Vancouver, who charted the coast in 1792. Captain George Vancouver's discovery of the Columbia River encouraged Thomas Jefferson and others to plan the Lewis and Clark expedition across the continental divide.

deal of exploring in this era and had more knowledge of geography than did the self-sufficient and relatively isolated Suquamish tribe.

As Sealth grew older, he was to see more ships, white explorers and settlers, and trade come to the Puget Sound. These strange and marvelous visitors would change his culture forever—including changing the ways in which its members communicated. By the time his name was first recorded as Seattle, in a Hudson's Bay Company log, he had become known as an intelligent and formidable leader whose agreement was sought for treaties and other documents. During this period of relatively harmonious dealings with the Salish, Chief Seattle made many overtures to white settlers. One man's account of meeting Chief Seattle was published in the *Oregon Spectator* newspaper, and his description of the chief's willingness to cooperate with settlers encouraged many people to migrate to the Oregon Valley during that decade.

Seattle actively sought out settlers with whom he could do business and trade, and he took up residence at Olympia to develop contacts and businesses. The latter were such a success that Americans who took claims near the native village of Dzidzula'lich on the east shore of the bay named the hybrid settlement Seattle after their patron and protector. However, his efforts to blend his people's future with the settlers' fell victim to land hunger and the desire of many influential whites to keep their people separate from the native population.

This, however, did not lessen Chief Seattle's friendship and loyalty. Notes from the translation of his speech greeting the prospect of treaty negotiations in January 1854 were purportedly written down by Henry Smith, a recent arrival to the area. It is the only written record of what must have been a remarkable speech by Chief Seattle, who was already known for his compelling voice, dignified bearing, and wise counsel. The story of Smith's article and of Chief Seattle's speech illustrates some of the difficulties outsiders face in trying to interpret Native American languages.

Smith said that the translation he produced "contained none of the grace and elegance of the original." His version began as follows:

Yonder sky that has wept tears of compassion upon my people for
centuries untold, and which to us appears changeless and eternal,
may change. Today is fair. Tomorrow it may be overcast with clouds.

13

My words are like the stars that never change. Whatever Seattle says, the great chief at Washington can rely upon with as much certainty as he can upon the return of the sun or the seasons.

In the 1970s, a writer named Ted Perry retranslated Chief Seattle's speech. The more modern version began:

How can you buy or sell the sky, the warmth of the land? The idea is strange to us. If we do not own the freshness of the air and the sparkle of the water, how can you buy them?

Every part of this earth is sacred to my people. Every shining pine needle, every sandy shore, every mist in the dark woods, every clearing and humming insect is holy in the memory and experience of my people. The sap which courses through the trees carries the memories of the red man.

Clearly, these two versions of Chief Seattle's speech are quite different. Perry has said that his version, used in an environmental film, was never meant to be anything but fiction. However, once people heard these words attributed to the Suquamish leader, they began to believe that Chief Seattle had made a speech in support of conserving land and resources. Many people, including presidents of the United States, have quoted Perry's "How can you buy the sky?" speech, as it is known, in support of ecological efforts. A popular children's book published in 1992 called *Brother Eagle, Sister Sky* creates a poetic version of Perry's words. However, neither of these versions was actually spoken by Chief Seattle.

Because of Seattle's importance as a native leader, he served as the native spokesman during the **treaty** council held at Point Elliott (Muckilteo) from December 27, 1854, to January 9, 1855. Despite voicing misgivings about his people receiving money for their land, he was the first to place his mark on the treaty **ceding** title to some 2.5 million acres of land, retaining a reservation for his fellow Suquamish but none for another local tribe, the Duwamish.

Unhappiness over the treaties and American arrogance caused many Duwamish to **repudiate** Seattle's leadership and led, ultimately, to the Yakima Indian War of 1855–57. He remained a firm **ally** of the Americans, but after the native forces were defeated, Seattle struggled to help his people. He retained his friendships with white settlers and cultivated new ones. Unable to live within the town that bears his name because of an **ordinance** forbidding permanent Indian houses within the city limits, he lived at his home on the Port Madison Reservation, north of the city limits.

Chief Seattle died on June 6, 1862. From the time of his first contact with Europeans to his death on the reservation, his world had changed dramatically and irreversibly. These changes would affect every aspect of Salish life, including the Lushootseed language they spoke. Today, only 100-200 **fluent** speakers of Lushootseed remain in a population of 500-600 Salish people. Ƨ

15

2 A Land of Many Tongues

The story of Chief Seattle and his tribe's first contact with white settlers reminds us of the many other stories of Native Americans in our nation's history. The returned slave Squanto helped the English Pilgrims communicate with the Wampanoags and thus learn to cultivate food for survival. Pocahontas, daughter of a Powhatan chieftain, met members of the Jamestown expedition and is reported to have saved John Smith's life by intervening when her father ordered his execution. Teenaged Shoshone tribeswoman Sacagawea played a vital role as translator in the Lewis and Clark expedition. There are many others, some whose names are known, and many others whose identity is lost in the mists of history.

The Pilgrims who landed in Massachusetts would probably not have survived the first year of settlement, had it not been for the Pawtuxet Indian Squanto. Squanto befriended the Pilgrims, taught them how to plant crops that would thrive in the soil, and served as an interpreter between the Europeans and his tribe's chief, Massasoit.

Squanto, whom we know as a great help to the English Pilgrim colony, learned English because a member of Captain John Smith's 1614 expedition that explored the coast of New England kidnapped him into slavery. After Squanto was brought back to the New World, he was captured during a battle and sent into the custody of the Wampanoag chief Massasoit. The chief sent Squanto as one of his representatives to the English Pilgrim settlers.

When learning about these historic figures, it may be difficult to comprehend how different they all were. Each of the people described lived in a different region, belonged to a different tribe, and spoke a different language. Squanto could not have carried on a conversation with Sacagawea. In fact, he might not even have been able to converse with a member of a tribe a few miles away.

In 1492, there were at least 350 different languages spoken by the Native Americans north of Mexico, including Inuits and Aleuts. These are totals of separate languages—not **dialects**. The speakers of one language could not understand any of the other languages without specifically learning them. If the different dialects of each of these languages were to be included, the totals would be much greater. Generally, separate tribes spoke separate languages. Imagine driving to the town next to yours and not being able to ask for directions. Even if the Native American tribes of the 15th century lived close together and belonged to the same tribal families, their members might have had difficulty exchanging the simplest information.

However, many Indian languages are related, just as English and

German are related, or Latin and French, and ultimately are linked to a single ancestral language. (English is a member of the Indo-European language family.) There were about 60 such language families north of Mexico and an even larger number in Latin America. The wide diversity that exists among many of the Native American languages is similar to that found among English, Hungarian, Arabic, Malay, and Chinese in Europe and Asia—all of which have different ancestral roots.

No Native American language comes from a historically known Old World language. The native languages of the Americas are

The most familiar story about Pocahontas is probably not even true. The leader of the English colonists at Jamestown, Virginia, John Smith, claimed that the young daughter of Chief Powhatan saved him from being put to death. However, this is probably an exaggeration. Pocahontas did help the struggling settlers through gifts of food and kindness.

Matoaks als Rebecka daughter to the mighty Prince Powhatan Emperour of Attanoughkomouck als Virginia converted and baptized in the Christian faith, and Wife to the wor.ll Mr Tho: Rolff.

She eventually married an English tobacco planter named John Rolfe and went to England, where she died in 1617.

presumed to have roots reaching back across Alaska's Bering Strait to the continent of Asia, but those roots date back to a remote period in the past. Furthermore, there is no direct evidence that this is indeed the case. The changes over the many thousands of years since the ancestors of the Old and New World peoples drifted apart have been so great that it is impossible to determine which ancestral language they might share.

When we begin to learn about Native American languages, the sheer number of them is one difficulty. An even greater difficulty is that much of what we know about these languages comes from settlers. When the first Europeans arrived on the Atlantic coast of the American continent, their civilization had already developed languages in their written form. Grammars had been developed and recorded for these languages, as well as methods for cataloguing changes in vocabulary and usage. The Native Americans used few written forms of speech, preferring an oral tradition for passing down knowledge. Although many forms of Native American languages were highly sophisticated (for example, the sign language used on the Great Plains), none of them was printed on a page in a book.

European settlers soon set about changing this state of affairs. Their reasons for doing so varied. Many explorers, like John Smith, were curious about every aspect of the land and people in the New World and wished to record the things they saw. Generally speaking, the earlier a tribe encountered white settlers, the earlier they began to lose aspects of their original language. Since most Europeans first came to the eastern shoreline territories, the tribes along the east coast were both the first to have their languages recorded and the first whose languages began to be lost.

Many of the first Native Americans encountered by Europeans belonged to tribes

Roger Williams, a minister, disagreed with the Puritans of Massachusetts and fled to Narragansett lands in search of religious freedom. He named his new settlement "Providence" in thanks to his God. That city is still the capital of the state of Rhode Island.

whose languages are no longer spoken, or are **extinct**. For example, the founder of Rhode Island, Roger Williams, originally settled this small territory with the idea of providing complete religious freedom for its inhabitants. Once there, he met members of the Narragansett tribe. Williams' *Dictionary of Narragansett* was the first attempt by a European to write down a Native American language. Williams went beyond vocabulary, however, and described the Narragansett tribe's appearance, objects, and customs.

According to tribal historians, the first documented contact between the Narragansett and whites took place in 1524, when Italian explorer Giovanni da Verrazano visited Narragansett Bay and described a large Indian population that lived by agriculture and hunting, and was organized under powerful "kings."

NATIVE AMERICAN LIFE

In 1524, the French king Francis I sent an Italian sailor named Giovanni da Verrazano to explore the newly discovered continent of North America. Verrazano investigated more than a thousand miles of Atlantic coastline, from North Carolina to Newfoundland. Verrazano was impressed with the Native Americans he met during his voyage. He described the men of one tribe as being larger than the Europeans. "[T]hey are of the color of brass, some of them incline more to whiteness: others are of yellow color . . . with long and black hair, which they are very careful to trim and deck up... The women are of the like conformity and beauty: very handsome and well favored, of pleasant countenance, and comely to behold...well mannered...and of good education."

The Narragansett escaped the **smallpox** plague that devastated other Native American tribes in the Northeast around 1617. At that point, their numbers increased because bands of refugees from disease-ridden areas joined them. Diseases brought by the Europeans were a major cause of death and tribal extinction, and the Narragansett did not completely escape this fate. In 1633, the tribe lost 700 members in a smallpox epidemic. In 1636, Roger Williams settled among them and, through cooperation, laid the foundations of the present-day state of Rhode Island. The Narragansett remained on good terms with the whites until King Philip's War (1675–76), into which they threw their whole strength. Afterwards, the rest of the tribe was forced to abandon the country. Some probably joined the Mahican and Abenaki, or even got as far as Canada and never returned to their own people; but others obtained permission to come back and settled among the Niantic tribe, which had taken no part in the contest. From that time on, the combined tribes were known as Narragansett. In 1788, many of these united with the Brotherhood Indians in New York, and a few went to live with the Mohegan in Connecticut. The remainder moved near Charlestown, Rhode Island.

Today in New England only three Native American languages are still spoken. In Maine, Abenaki-Penobscot and Malecite-Passamaquoddy are spoken by about 200 and 1,100 people, respectively. These people live primarily on reservation lands. In New York and Boston, members of reservation communities speak the Micmac language. Most of the Eastern and Atlantic coast native languages belonged to the Algonquian family. The languages in this family stretched from the Passamaquoddy of Maine to the Carolina Algonquians and included Massachuset (Massachusetts), Abenaki (throughout northern New England), Mohegan (New York), Lenape (Delaware), Nanticoke (Maryland), and Powhatan (Virginia). §

23

NATIVE AMERICAN LIFE

A KEY into the

LANGUAGE

OF

AMERICA:

OR,

An help to the *Language* of the *Natives* in that part of AMERICA, called *NEW-ENGLAND*.

Together, with briefe *Observations* of the Cuſtomes, Manners and Worſhips, &c. of the aforeſaid *Natives*, in Peace and Warre, in Life and Death.

On all which are added Spirituall *Observations*, Generall and Particular by the *Authour*, of chiefe and ſpeciall uſe (upon all occaſions,) to all the *Engliſh* Inhabiting thoſe parts; yet pleaſant and profitable to the view of all men:

BY ROGER WILLIAMS
of *Providence* in *New-England*.

LONDON,
Printed by *Gregory Dexter*, 1643.

3 Building New Worlds and New Words

One historian of Native America has pointed out that when the first Europeans came to America, they saw a great many new things: trees, plants, foodstuffs, fish, birds, and animals. They had no way to express these new sights and objects, so they often adopted words from the Native American tribes in the area. Our language contains many of these, which are known as **loan words**. Our language also contains many ideas borrowed from Indian languages and set down in English, which are known as **Indianisms**.

Patterns as to which kinds of words were borrowed and how many were borrowed in a particular time period depend on several historical factors. As President Thomas Jefferson noted, "new circumstances" called for "new words," and the first sets of loan words reflect the physical circumstances of the New World. One of the earliest European visitors, Englishman James Rosier, recorded the Native American words "moose" and "caribou" for two new animals that he saw. Famed explorer John Smith contributed "raccoon," from the Virginia Algonquian "aroughcun," to common usage. Words for trees and plants were also heavily borrowed from Indian allies. For example, Smith also noted the words "hickory" and "persimmon."

Later loan words have more to do with Indian culture and how European settlers chose to see it and use it. Words for housing, clothing, foodstuffs, and tools became familiar. Moccasin, tepee, and maize came from eastern and midwestern tribes; igloo, pone, and umiak came from western and northern tribes.

As European Americans became more comfortable with the idea of Native American culture (although not necessarily with Native Americans), they began to develop new ways to use native languages. Instead of using Native American nouns as nouns, they would take a loan word and use it as a different part of speech. A good example of this is the verb we use to describe the noise a goose makes—honk. "Honck" is a Wampanoag word for goose; its first recorded use as a verb is in Henry David Thoreau's book *Walden*, in which he describes a "honking goose."

Another interesting example that has not been fully proved is the origin of our common term "okay." There are many ideas about where this word came from, but one possibility is that settlers began using the Choctaw word "oke," meaning "it is so." The Choctaw tribe used this word to signify that two parties were in agreement. Today, we use the word "okay" for much the same reason.

One historian points out that a famous term for early colonists may have come from a Cherokee word meaning "slave" or "coward." The Cherokee "eankke" is pronounced much like "Yankee," and could have been an insulting term heard and then used by English settlers for those who opposed rule by the British monarchy.

The colonists in the New World borrowed many words from the Native American languages to describe new plants and animals. The word "goose" was used to refer to animals similar to ducks, but with heavier bodies and longer necks. The male goose is called a gander, and an immature goose is a gosling.

Seattle is the largest city in Washington State,
with a population of over 500,000. Named
after Chief Seattle, one of the original
inhabitants, the area and the people living
there have changed considerably since the
establishment of the city.

The original "Yankees" named many of their states and cities after places in their home country (New York, after the city of York and county of Yorkshire), or created names to honor their founders (Pennsylvania, established by William Penn). As colonists moved farther and farther west, more and more states, cities, rivers, and mountain ranges were given names derived from local tribes.

Twenty-six of our 50 states have Native American names. These are (in alphabetical order): Alabama, Alaska, Arizona, Arkansas, Connecticut, Idaho, Illinois, Iowa, Kansas, Kentucky, Massachusetts, Michigan, Minnesota, Mississippi, Missouri, Nebraska, New Mexico, North Dakota, Ohio, Oklahoma, South Dakota, Tennessee, Texas, Utah, Wisconsin, and Wyoming. Cities have also received Native American names. Chicago, Miami, and Seattle are just three examples. Sometimes cities were named after tribes, as in the case of the Miami people of Florida; sometimes they were named after famous Native Americans, as in the case of Chief Seattle.

Far greater than the number of states or cities given Native American names is the number of smaller places, including lakes, rivers, creeks, and ponds. The "Mighty Mississippi" has a Native American name, as does its sister river, the Missouri. Lake Michigan of the Great Lakes has a Native American name, as does New York's Saranac Lake in the Adirondack Mountains—another Native American name. Several mountain ranges carry Native American names—for example, the Appalachians.

Many cities and towns in the United States have streets, parks, and other facilities with Indian names. At Fort Leavenworth, Kansas, the

29

NATIVE AMERICAN LIFE

> **Vocabulary changes along with history. Today, we avoid phrases that might once have been known as "Indianisms," such as "Indian giver," "going on the warpath," "let's have a powwow," "paleface," "redskin," and so on.**

housing areas for army personnel have names like Pawnee Village and Kansa Village. Many Indian place-names have been translated into English, such as Battle Creek, or into French, such as Baton Rouge.

Translating Native American words and phrases into English has resulted in a large number of Indianisms in American vocabulary. While it was sometimes easy to adopt a Native American term, as in the case of moccasin, at other times, settlers felt more comfortable describing new things in their native tongue. The crop of corn, which some early settlers called "maize," from the Central American Taino language, sustained colonists in the New World. However, the word "corn" is actually an Old English term for grain. The settlers began calling their new foodstuff "Indian corn" in order to distinguish it as part of their new surroundings.

Other phrases using "Indian" include "Indian summer," which describes a period in the fall of mild and often sunny weather. This time of year had different names back in Europe. A 19th-century newspaper article noted that settlers may have chosen to call it Indian summer because it was the time of year when tribes began to prepare for winter hunting.

Many Native American tribes, especially those of the Far North like the Inuit, have depended on hunting caribou for meat and hides. Settlers borrowed the word "caribou" from Native Americans to refer to the unfamiliar animal.

31

Many Indianisms were coined to describe Native American ways and culture. A "longhouse" referred to a type of dwelling common among the Algonquian tribes. Both "warpath" and "peace pipe," terms used in very different circumstances, are Indianisms.

Native American loan words and Indianisms serve as reminders of moments in our nation's history in which contact was made and both white and **indigenous** peoples communicated. While the actual "borrowing" between languages peaked in the late 19th century, words like caucus, hickory, and wigwam remain in our modern vocabulary. ⑤

The Shoshone woman Sacagawea attempts to communicate with members of another tribe as the members of the Lewis and Clark expedition paddle down the lower Columbia River. Sacagawea was a useful guide because she was able to communicate with some of the other Indian groups the American explorers encountered on their 1804–06 journey to the Pacific. Even without speaking, however, her presence with the party sent an important message to the tribes Lewis and Clark encountered: their intentions were peaceful, for a war party would not include a woman with a small child.

 **Great Communication Divides**

In 1836, U.S. Secretary of War Albert Gallatin began the first attempt to create a comprehensive scheme of American Indian languages, as they were called at the time. Gallatin took on this project because the Department of War was responsible for negotiations with Native American tribes and needed to know as many ways to communicate with them as possible.

Gallatin revised and expanded his scheme in 1848, and subsequent attempts to classify Native American languages have been made that include the indigenous languages of both North and South America. Many scholars of languages, or **linguists**, disagree, however, on how such a classification should be made. Some (known as traditionalists) often have dozens of language families in their schemes because they believe direct relationships between many of these families have not been made. Others (known as reductionists) try to limit the number of language families in order to show their close relationships.

The arguments between these two groups of scholars are complex, but they point to something significant. Until recently, university-level study of Native American languages was carried out by Americans of European descent rather than by native speakers of those languages.

Swiss-born Albert Gallatin served as Secretary of the Treasury under Presidents Madison and Jefferson. He worked to reduce the public debt, surveyed all available transportation routes in the United States, and worked to create a comprehensive knowledge of Native American languages across the continent.

The history of Europeans' warfare with and persecution of Native Americans resulted in Indian languages being downplayed and, in many cases, drowned out. Pressures on different tribal groups to adopt languages of European origin resulted in fewer and fewer people learning those languages at an early age.

Since only a handful of Native American languages have written histories, most of our study materials are quite recent. However, we do know that the large number of languages and dialects differ greatly in their structures.

Studying these sounds and making comparisons among them is the primary method scholars have for establishing relationships between Native American languages. When a connection is made, languages can be grouped into families, which can then be classified into phyla (or stocks), and then into macrophyla (superstocks). Reconstructing these language ties can help anthropologists, historians, and others to learn more about the people who spoke them.

The number of Native American language families increases from east to west in North America. Historian Lyle Campbell points out that 3 major families exist in the East, but 20 are found in California alone. After encountering the Algonquian languages (that is, Wampanoag, Narragansett, Iroquois) in the East and Muskogean languages (Chocktaw-Chickasaw) in the Southeast, settlers would have heard languages from the Siouan (Assiniboin or Dakota/Lakota and Winnebago) and Caddo (Wichita) families. Next, they would have heard Uto-Aztecan family languages, such as Hopi Pueblo and Papago.

In the northwest coastal region, Shoshonean, Salishan, and Chinookan language families are distinct from their Californian neighbors and the northern Inuit-Aleut language family. In total, there are about 55 independent language families in North America. Contrast that number with just 15 in Middle America and 115 in South America!

Tribal names can be confusing when someone is trying to distinguish language groups. Some names were chosen for linguistic reasons, but others were created to show separation between groups. For example, Creek and Seminole, both Muskogean family languages, are mutually **intelligible**, but the tribes who use them are different. Furthermore, some tribal names are derived from foreign languages, like the English name "Dog Rib" for a particular Athabascan tribe or the French name "Gros Ventre" (literally, "large belly").

35

NATIVE AMERICAN LIFE

Tribal names can be descriptive, too. Many tribes use their language or dialect's word for "people" as their name—for example, Wampanoag means "earth people." The names of others indicate specific types of people. Hunkpapa means "campers at the opening of the circle"; Mohawk means "possessors of the flint." Other tribal names describe a group and represent a symbol for them. For example, Iroquois means "people of the extended lodge" or "snake." The Pawnee "look like wolves," and the Salish are "flatheads." These tribes may have been given their names by neighbors. Still other names describe actions (Alabama means "I clear the thicket") or the region in which the tribe lives (Seneca means "place of stone").

From the variety of these names, it is evident that while Native American languages can be quite different, none could be called **primitive**. There are specific rules of **grammar** and **syntax** in Native American languages; furthermore, there are specific sounds in these languages. According to historian Lyle Campbell, the Mohawk language has 15 distinct sounds, while Shoshone has 49 (American English has 40). As they encountered all of these distinct rules and sounds, European settlers often chose to ignore or destroy them. Speakers of Inuit-Aleut were forbidden to use their native tongue at

Symbols in Native American sign language usually had a clear relation to the thing they represented: an object's form, an action's movement, or the placement of an item.

This hide painting, created by the Shoshone tribe of the Great Plains, depicts a buffalo dance after the hunt. Because of the absence of a written language, hide paintings were one important way tribal history and culture was passed along to younger generations.

37

school or in public. Without education in their language, these people soon lost their ability to use it.

Two other Native American communication methods deserve special mention: jargon/**pidgin** language, represented by Chinook Jargon, and Indian sign language.

Chinook Jargon is a trade language that was used extensively in the 19th century and first part of the 20th century for communication between Europeans and Native Americans in much of the Pacific Northwest, including British Columbia. Chinook Jargon is part of a family of trade languages known as "pidgins" that allow people from different cultures to communicate quickly and effectively. Besides Chinook Jargon, pidgins in the Americas include Mednyj Aleut, Michif (or French Cree), and Lingua Geral Amazonica in Brazil.

Chinook Jargon is a language with a simplified grammar that draws its vocabulary from several other languages. The largest parts of its vocabulary come from Chinook and Nuuchanuulth, followed by French. It also contains words from other native languages and from English. Some of its vocabulary is simple and mimics natural sounds— for example, "tiktik" means watch, and "liplip" echoes the sound water makes when boiling. In jargon languages, words can have multiple meanings even without changes in spelling or **intonation**. In Chinook Jargon, "wawa" can mean ask, talk, gossip, narrate, or even message, conversation, legend, and question—among other meanings.

American Indian sign language became a common means of communication for Great Plains tribes who spoke different languages. Using signs made almost entirely with the hands and fingers, this became a highly developed language of its own. William Tomkins, who learned sign language from Sioux Indians in the late 19th and early 20th centuries, compiled a book about its vocabulary and use. He

A Native American on horseback raises his open hand in a sign of peace. Because there were hundreds of different Native American languages and dialects, the members of native tribes often had to use universally understood hand gestures to communicate.

39

noted that the most practiced "speakers" of Indian sign language used fluid movements as they changed from one sign to another. "It has a beauty and imagery possessed by few, if any, other languages. It is the foremost gesture language the world has ever produced." S

5 A New Land with an Old Language

This book primarily discusses native languages of the part of North America known as the United States. However, there are many other native languages in the Americas. For example, in South America, before the arrival of European settlers, over 1,500 native languages were spoken; about 350 of these survive today. More information about these modern native languages is provided in the following chapter.

In this chapter, another part of North America and its native tongue will be examined: Nunavut. Nunavut is a new province of Canada, formed in 1999 from that country's northernmost regions. The native people living in the Northwest Territory had long wished for their own borders and ability to govern. It took many years for political negotiations to be made, but on April 1, 1999, Nunavut became the first territory to enter the federation of Canada since Newfoundland

A majority of the people living in the new Canadian province of Nunavut are Inuit. Over the past 100 years the Inuit have attempted to preserve their language and culture while adapting to modern life.

> **The Inuktitut word for ice is "siku," and there are 18 different words for different ice conditions, such as rough ice, sea ice, and iceberg.**

in 1949. Although Nunavut is subject to the Canadian Constitution and its Charter of Rights and Freedoms, its population reflects an older sensibility.

What does that mean? The population of Nunavut (which means "the land" in the Inuktitut language) is 85 percent Inuit (which means "the people" in the Inuktitut language). The Inuit are an indigenous people whose tribes range from Chukotka in Russia to Greenland, making them the only North American people whose language ranges over two continents. Once known by the Cree Indian word "Eskimo," meaning "eaters of raw meat," the Inuit consider this term derogatory and old-fashioned, preferring instead to use their name for themselves.

One Inuit journalist says that the changes the Inuit have faced over the past 100 years are equivalent to those European nations had to face over the past 5,000 years. The Inuit use one word to mean both culture and habits. The meaning of this word includes living a life based on the land, the weather, and the sea. Because Inuit tradition is oral, these elements of the culture were inseparable from Inuktitut. Of the Inuit generations now living, the oldest grew up speaking only Inuktitut and living a **nomadic** life as hunters, fishers, and plant gatherers.

An Inuit performs a folk dance. Children are
still taught in their native language in
Canadian and Alaskan schools to ensure their
rich culture does not fade away.

The first **bilingual** Inuits, now in their mid-thirties and forties, learned Inuktitut at home and English at school. While this "in-the-middle" group still experienced many of the old ways, their younger counterparts have seen much less of country living. Because they were losing their language, new efforts were made to teach Inuktitut in schools. While these efforts are still ongoing, they have had quite a bit of success.

From living on the land as hunter-gatherers to living in cities as industrial workers, the Inuit have adapted to modern life while still maintaining their own culture and language. Inuktitut will be the official working language of the new territorial government, with English and French also being used. While dialects and accents can vary from region to region, Inuktitut is considered a single language. In the Baffin and Kivalliq regions, Inuktitut is written in a system called **syllabics**. This symbol-like alphabet was developed by a minister for the Cree language and adapted for Inuktitut by an Anglican missionary named Edmund Peck. Peck fashioned its symbols after secretarial shorthand.

In the western part of Nunavut's Kitikmeot region, Inuktitut is written using roman orthography—what we know as our western alphabet. Using roman orthography, it is easy to see that in Inuktitut, a single word can be spelled many different ways. For example, the word meaning "white person" can be written "qallunaq" or "kabloona"—the words are pronounced the same way—"kah-BLUE-nah." Perhaps it was these varied spellings that led to one of the most common misconceptions about Inuktitut: that "the Eskimos" have dozens and dozens of words for snow! In fact, Inuktitut has one word for snow: "aput." However, the language does have many different ways of describing different kinds of snow: wet, dry, powdery, icy—no surprise in a climate that experiences snow almost every day of the year.

Baffin and Kivalliq, the eastern regions of Nunavut, have many more speakers of Inuktitut. In the mid-19th century, the language was relatively pure. As more and more Westerners moved to the region, however, more and more changes were made to Inuktitut. When the Hudson's Bay Company, the most prominent merchandiser in Canada, moved to the Inuit lands, words like coffee, tea, sugar, flour, and paper were introduced. Inuit journalist Ann Meekitjuk Hanson notes that while these words became common, they were given Inuit pronunciations—for example, "tea" became "tii" and "sugar" became "sukaq."

The last speaker of Eyak, a language related to Inuit, was Marie Smith. She died in 2000 at the age of 82.

45

Inuktitut has a regular grammatical system that is as precise as it is complex. The language uses word building, but combines this with a "pretty sophisticated approach to word definition," according to Inuit teacher Alexina Kublu. Objects are described by their function rather than by their appearance. Some native languages might describe a helicopter as a "flying metal bird," but in Inuktitut, it is known as "qulimiguulik," meaning "that which has something going through the space above itself."

SOME COMMON INUKTITUT PHRASES AND THEIR PRONUNCIATIONS

How are you?	*Qanuippit?* (Khah-nweep-peet)
I am fine.	*Qanuinngittunga.* (Khah-nwee-nngit-toonga)
What is your name?	*Kinauvit?* (Kee-nah-oo-veet)
Thank you.	*Qujannamiik.* (Khoo-yannah-meek)
You are welcome.	*Ilaali.* (E-laah-li)
Yes.	*Ii.* (Ee)
No.	*Aakka.* (Ah-ka)
Maybe.	*Immaqqaa.* (Eem-mak-haw)
Good-bye. (to an individual)	*Tavvauvutit.* (Tub-vow-voo-teet)
Good-bye. (to a group)	*Tavvauvusi.* (Tub-vow-voo-see)

After the introduction of written Inuktitut, it was somewhat easier to make new terms and phrases fit in with the language. At the same time, fewer and fewer children were learning Inuktitut at school. New programs have reversed this trend, and now more and more people in Nunavut are conversant in Inuktitut. In western Nunavut, however, the situation is more serious. Efforts to revive Inuktitut (or any dying language) are called "**salvage linguistics**."

Meekitjuk Hanson writes, "Today we may not use the traditional terms our fathers used when hunting, navigating, or creating new tools, but we have created new terms for the technology that is available to us." Terms for new technology items like computers, televisions, satellites, and the Internet are translated into Inuktitut rather than simply pronounced in the local way. Although it will take more time and effort before Inuktitut is again established as the common language of Nunavut, this translation signifies a new awareness of Inuktitut's strength and usefulness. ⑤

This bronze sculpture in Phoenix, Arizona, memorializes the Navajo Code Talkers of World War II. The use of the Navajo language to send messages between Allied troops helped bring about a victory in the war.

Native American Languages Today

When Columbus landed in the New World in 1492, more than 300 separate Native American languages were spoken in what is now the United States. Today, that number has been reduced to 175.

Yet that doesn't mean the 175 languages are spoken by many people. About 20 of these languages are still spoken in homes by children, meaning that these languages are still taught by their parents. Most of these 20 languages, like Navajo, Hopi, and Western Apache, are spoken in New Mexico and Arizona.

Approximately 30 of the surviving Native American languages are spoken by parents and **elders** in Montana, Iowa, and Alaska, including Crow, Cheyenne, and Jicarilla Apache. Far more numerous are the 70 languages spoken only by elders in California, Alaska, Oregon, Maine, and Washington. These languages, which include Tlingit, Winnebago, Comanche, Yuma, and Yakima, are mainly spoken on reservation lands. Fewer than 10 elders can speak 55 other languages, such as Mandan and Pawnee—mostly in California, Washington, Iowa, and North Dakota.

After decades of increasing language loss among Native American peoples, the U.S. government approved the 1990 Native American

After 12 years of work, Chief Sequoyah invented the Cherokee alphabet and writing system in 1821. This system not only made his people able to read and write, but also allowed white colonists to translate between English and Cherokee.

Cherokee Alphabet.

D a	R e	T i	Ꭷ o	O u	i v
S ga Ꭺ ka	Ᏺ ge	Ᏻ gi	A go	J gu	E gv
Ꮖ ha	Ᏸ he	Ꭾ hi	Ꮂ ho	Ꮁ hu	Ꮒ hv
W la	Ꮈ le	Ꮅ li	Ꮆ lo	M lu	Ꮭ lv
Ꮉ ma	Ꮋ me	H mi	Ꮍ mo	Ꮽ mu	
Ꮎ na Ꮏ hna Ꮐ nah	Ꮑ ne	Ꮒ ni	Z no	Ꮗ nu	Ꮕ nv
Ꮙ qua	Ꮖ que	Ꮗ qui	Ꮚ quo	Ꮘ quu	Ꮜ quv
U sa Ꮝ s	Ꮞ se	Ꮟ si	Ꮠ so	Ꮡ su	R sv
Ꮣ da Ꮤ ta	Ꮥ de Ꮦ te	Ꮧ di Ꮨ ti	V do	Ꮪ du	Ꮫ dv
Ꮬ dla Ꮮ tla	Ꮯ tle	Ꮳ tli	Ꮴ tlo	Ꮵ tlu	Ꮅ tlv
Ꮶ tsa	Ꮷ tse	Ꮸ tsi	Ꮹ tso	Ꮺ tsu	Ꮻ tsv
Ꮻ wa	Ꮼ we	Ꮖ wi	Ꮼ wo	Ꮽ wu	6 wv
Ꮿ ya	Ᏸ ye	Ᏹ yi	Ᏺ yo	Ᏻ yu	B yv

In May 2001, Hulilauakea Wilson graduated from high school. He was the first native Hawaiian in 100 years to have been educated exclusively in the Hawaiian language.

Languages Act. In this bill, the status of cultures and languages of Native Americans is deemed "unique," and the U.S. acknowledges a shared responsibility with Native Americans to help these things survive.

But, as Dr. Richard Littlebear (a Cheyenne) writes, "Why save our languages, since they now seem to have no political, economic, or global relevance?" Many people believe that old languages should die out. After all, we can all communicate in English, and there is no need for small groups of people to speak little-known dialects that can be difficult to master.

Littlebear answers his own question by saying, "It is the spiritual relevance deeply embedded in our own languages that makes them relevant to us as Indians today." The Native American Languages Act echoes these words by stating that, "Languages are the means of communication for the full range of human experiences and are critical to the survival of cultural and political integrity of any people."

Kenneth Hale, a linguist at the Massachusetts Institute of Technology, said, "When you lose a language, it's like dropping a bomb on a museum." When a language dies, information about a culture is lost forever. Modern linguists say that about four languages disappear every two months, and at that rate, half of the world's existing 6,000-plus languages will be gone by the next century. Over half of these existing

A woman named Frances Densmore uses a wax
cylinder phonograph to record the native language of
the Blackfoot Indians in 1916. Had scholars not taken
an interest in native languages when they did, many of
the subtleties of the cultures may have been lost.

This Mayan temple was built more than 1,500 years ago. Although the classic period of Mayan civilization ended around A.D. 900, native people living in Mexico, Honduras, and Guatemala still speak the language.

languages are spoken in nine countries, including India and China. Only 5 to 10 percent of these existing languages are considered entirely secure.

Not everyone believes that losing languages is bad. Some people say that it is natural to lose languages over time. Others, however, believe that the increasing rate of language loss around the world points to what was mentioned earlier: languages dying because of intervention from members of dominant cultures who believed their own cultures and languages were superior.

Reversing the prejudices against Native American languages that began early on in our nation's history is not an easy task. The government enacted policies to prevent them from being handed down from generation to generation. An 1868 federal report called Native American languages "barbarous" and said they should be "blotted out and the English language substituted."

Until the 1990 Native American Languages Act, the government was all-too-successful in carrying out this task. A 79-year-old Cahuilla tribeswoman named Katherine Silva Saubel is the last fluent speaker of her native tongue. On her reservation in California, she recalled for a journalist what it was like to grow up in the United States speaking a Native American language. She heard no English until the age of

55

seven, when she was sent to a public school: "I don't remember when I began to understand what was being said to me . . . maybe [after] a year." She saw other Native American classmates whipped for speaking their language at school.

Nevertheless, Saubel loved to learn and became the first Indian

The Navajo Nation has 80,000 native speakers and maintains its own college-level training to produce teachers of Navajo for 240 schools in Arizona, New Mexico, and Utah with large numbers of Navajo students.

woman to graduate from Palm Springs High School and also to become an **ethnobotanist**. In her later years, she has been both the subject of linguistic research and a caretaker of her culture and language. "My race is dying," Saubel told the *L.A. Times* newspaper. "I am saving the remnants of my culture." She has produced a dictionary of Cahuilla and recorded songs and vocabulary. She founded the Makli Museum, the first in North America to be organized, managed, and maintained by Native Americans, and there houses her memorabilia along with tribal **artifacts**.

While Saubel's efforts are positive, many other efforts to save Native American languages encounter problems. For example, many Native Americans find themselves more comfortable speaking in English—especially when modern vocabulary is involved. If words can't be expressed in a Native American language, people fall back on English. Many Native American language-education programs seek to replace English words for new ideas and objects with words in their own tongue. In the Northern Californian Karuk language, for example, wristwatch is defined as "little sun worn on the wrist."

On and off reservation lands there are now programs that teach Native American languages, and there are also programs of bilingual education so that the newest native speakers can learn English without losing their first language. Curricula in Navajo, Apache, and Salish—to name just a few—are in place. It is now possible to find dictionaries and grammars for many Native American languages in bookstores and online. Sadly, not all languages that are dying or extinct have been

An Apache woman makes the hand sign for "winter." Sign language was common among the native tribes of the Southwest, who spoke a variety of different languages.

57

recorded. Others, like Narragansett, may have just one dictionary or grammar written, and that is not widely available. The Natick tribe of Massachusetts had its language recorded in a dictionary that can now be found virtually only in Natick, Massachusetts.

There are many reasons why Native Americans wish to save their languages. Littlebear outlines several: ability to communicate, sovereignty, a sense of belonging, and spirituality. He writes, "The Cheyenne language is my language. English is also my language. Yet it is Cheyenne I want to use . . . when I greet those who've journeyed on before me [to the spirit world.]" §

NATIVE AMERICAN LIFE

GLOSSARY

ally one that is associated with another as a helper.

artifact something remaining from a human society.

bilingual able to use two languages equally well.

cede to yield or grant, typically by treaty.

dialects regional varieties of language distinguished by features of vocabulary, grammar, and pronunciation from other regional varieties and constituting together with them a single language.

elders members of a tribe holding authority by virtue of age and experience, who are usually accorded great respect.

ethnobotanist a person who studies the plant lore of a people.

extinct no longer existing.

fluent ready in speech.

grammar the study of the classes of words, their inflections, and their functions and relations in a sentence.

Indianisms words or phrases translated into English from Native American languages.

indigenous having originated in a particular region.

intelligible capable of being understood.

intonation the rise and fall in pitch of the voice in speech.

linguists people who specialize in the study of human speech, including units, nature, structure, and modification of language.

literacy the ability to read and write.

loan words words and phrases borrowed from Native American languages and used in their original state in the English language.

nomadic roaming about from place to place aimlessly, frequently, or without a fixed pattern of movement.

ordinance a law set forth by a government authority, often prescribing some sort of behavior.

pidgin a simplified speech used for communication between people with different languages.

primitive something that closely approximates an early ancestral type.

repudiate to refuse to accept.

salvage linguistics a branch of speech/language study devoted to saving languages in danger of becoming extinct.

smallpox a contagious disease characterized by a skin eruption with pustules, sloughing, and scar formation.

syllabics the sounds various syllables make, or symbols used to denote those sounds.

syntax the way in which words are put together to form phrases or clauses.

treaty an agreement or arrangement made between two political entities, formally signed by both.

NATIVE AMERICAN LIFE

FURTHER READING

Barnes, Ian. *Historical Atlas of Native Americans*. London: Cartographica Press, 2009.

Cutler, Charles L. *O Brave New Worlds!: Native American Loanwords in Current English*. Norman: University of Oklahoma Press, 1994.

Hoffman, Elizabeth DeLaney. *American Indians and Popular Culture*. 2 vols. Santa Barbara, Calif.: ABC-CLIO, 2012.

Jones, David, and Brian Molyneaux. *The Illustrated Encyclopedia of American Indian Mythology: Legends, Gods and Spirits of North, Central, and South America*. Leicester, U.K.: Anness, 2010.

Kroskrity, Paul V. and Margaret C. Field. *Native American Language Ideologies: Beliefs, Practices, and Struggles in Indian Country*. Tuscon: University of Arizona Press, 2009.

Page, Jake. *In the Hands of the Great Spirit: The 20,000-Year History of American Indians*. New York: Free Press, 2003.

Tomkins, William. *Indian Sign Language*. New York: Dover Publications, 2012.

Waldman, Carl. *Encyclopedia of Native American Tribes*. New York: Facts on File, 2006.

NATIVE AMERICAN LIFE

INTERNET RESOURCES

http://www.csulb.edu/colleges/cla/departments/americanindianstudies/faculty/trj/
Website of the American Indian Studies program at California State University, Long Beach, which is chaired by Professor Troy Johnson. The site presents unique artwork, photographs, video, and sound recordings that accurately reflect the rich history and culture of Native Americans.

http://www.terralingua.org
Terralingua is devoted to the conservation and preservation of world languages.

http://www.nativeculture.com/lisamitten/natlang.html
This site contains many links to other web pages related to Native American languages.

http://www.ailla.utexas.org/site/welcome.html
This is an online digital archive of audio and textual materials documenting the indigenous languages and cultures of Latin America.

http://www.cogsci.indiana.edu/farg/rehling/nativeAm/ling.html
This site contains information about native languages of North America.

http://www.native-languages.org/
Native Languages of the Americas is a small non-profit organization dedicated to the survival of Native American languages. The group's website includes links to information about more than 800 native languages.

NATIVE AMERICAN LIFE

INDEX

63

NATIVE AMERICAN LIFE

PICTURE CREDITS

CONTRIBUTORS

Dr. Troy Johnson is chairman of the American Indian Studies program at California State University, Long Beach, California. He is an internationally published author and is the author, co-author, or editor of twenty books, including *Wisdom Spirits: American Indian Prophets, Revitalization Movements, and Cultural Survival* (University of Nebraska Press, 2012); *The Indians of Eastern Texas and The Fredonia Revolution of 1828* (Edwin Mellen Press, 2011); and *The American Indian Red Power Movement: Alcatraz to Wounded Knee* (University of Nebraska Press, 2008). He has published numerous scholarly articles, has spoken at conferences across the United States, and is a member of the editorial board of the journals *American Indian Culture and Research and The History Teacher*. Dr. Johnson has served as president of the Society of History Education since 2001. He has won awards for his permanent exhibit at Alcatraz Island; he also was named Most Valuable Professor of the Year by California State University, Long Beach, in 1997 and again in 2006. He served as associate director and historical consultant on the award-winning PBS documentary film *Alcatraz Is Not an Island* (1999). Dr. Johnson lives in Long Beach, California.

Bethanne Kelly Patrick holds a master's degree in English from the University of Virginia and specializes in middle-school curricula. She is a freelance writer who lives with her husband and two daughters in Virginia.